The Twelve Labours of Heracles

Author:

James Ford studied English and Classics at Oxford University. He taught English in Greece before returning to England to work in publishing. He lives in Brighton.

Artist:

Peter Rutherford was born in Ipswich. He studied illustration and animation at Ipswich Art College and then worked as an Art Director in several leading London Advertising Agencies. He now lives and works in Suffolk and has been illustrating children's books for the past 10 years.

Series creator:

David Salariya was born in Dundee, Scotland. He has illustrated a wide range of books and has created and designed many new series for publishers both in the UK and overseas. In 1989, he established The Salariya Book Company. He lives in Brighton with his wife, illustrator Shirley Willis, and their son Jonathan.

Editor:

Michael Ford

Published in Great Britain in 2005 by
Book House, an imprint of
The Salariya Book Company Ltd
25 Marlborough Place, Brighton BN1 1UB

Please visit the Salariya Book Company at:
www.salariya.com
www.book-house.co.uk

ISBN 1 904642-34-9

A catalogue record for this book is available from the British Library.

Printed and bound in Malta.
Reprinted 2006

Printed on paper from sustainable forests.

Ancient Greek Myths

The Twelve Labours of Heracles

Written by
James Ford

Illustrated by
Peter Rutherford

Created and designed by
David Salariya

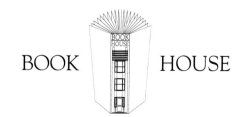

BOOK HOUSE

The world of Ancient Greek mythology

The Ancient Greek civilisation was one of the greatest the world has witnessed. It spanned nearly two thousand years, until it was eventually overwhelmed by the Roman Empire in the second century BC. At its height, the Greek world extended far beyond what we know as modern Greece.

We owe much to the Ancient Greeks. They were great scientists, mathematicians, dramatists and philosophers. They were also brilliant storytellers. Many of the tales they told were in the form of poetry, often thousands of lines long. The Greeks wrote poems about all kinds of human experience – love, friendship, war, revenge, history and even simple everyday activities. The most famous of the poems which have passed down to us are the epic tales of courage and warfare, where brave heroes struggle and suffer against great odds.

A map showing the Ancient Greek mainland, surrounding islands and neighbouring lands

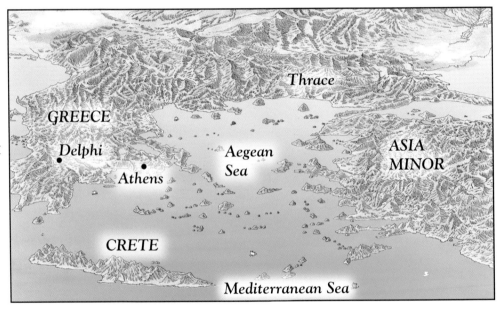

What is incredible is that until the eighth century BC, the Greeks had no recognised form of writing. All of their stories, lengthy as they were, were handed down from generation to generation by word of mouth. The people who passed on these tales were often professional storytellers, who would perform to music in town squares or public theatres. Often several versions of the same myth existed, depending on who told it and when. What follows is one version of the adventures of Heracles.

If you need help with any of the names, go to the pronunciation guide on page 31.

Introduction

Gather round and hear my story. I will tell you all of the greatest hero the world has ever seen. Of whom am I speaking? Why, Heracles of course! Storytellers of old say that he was the son of a beautiful woman called Alcmene, and the king of the Gods, Zeus. But just because his father was a god, it didn't mean that Heracles had an easy life. Zeus's wife, Hera, made sure of that. She was angry that Zeus had fathered a child with a mortal woman and she despised Heracles. In revenge, she cast a spell on him, which made him kill his wife and children. When Heracles realised the terrible crime he had committed, he asked the famous oracle at Delphi how he could pay for his dreadful crime. He was told to travel to the kingdom of Mycenae and visit King Eurystheus. Only by obeying the king's every command would Heracles ever be forgiven for killing his family.

I am the storyteller – lend me your ears!

The Nemean Lion

King Eurystheus was pleased to have a new servant to perform his every wish. For fun, he decided to set Heracles 12 impossible labours, or tasks, and looked forward to seeing the brave young man fail. First of these was to kill a ferocious lion in the land of Nemea. This fearsome creature had been devouring local people and terrorising the land. It lived in a deep cave with two entrances, so that it always had an escape route. Its skin was so thick that no sword could pierce it. Heracles soon found out that arrows were useless as well. He fired a whole quiver-full, but they all bounced off harmlessly. So the hero changed his tactics. Blocking off one of the entrances to the lion's den with a huge boulder, Heracles chased the beast inside. In this way he cornered the lion and wrestled it with his bare hands. After a great contest, Heracles strangled the savage beast.

Eurystheus and his jar

When Heracles returned to Eurystheus's kingdom with the dead lion, the king was so terrified that he hid in a *pithos*, a large jar made for storing food.

Ask the storyteller

What happened to the lion?

Not wanting to waste his prize, Heracles skinned the dead lion and wore its pelt over his body.

The Hydra of Lerna

King Eurystheus was embarrassed when he eventually emerged from his jar. He decided to set Heracles an even more difficult second task – to kill the Hydra. You will have to stretch your minds to imagine this terrible monster. It had the body of a dragon and nine heads, each with a ravenous mouth lined with sharp teeth. To find the Hydra, Heracles had to travel to the land of Lerna, and the swamp in which it lived.

Facing one enemy was hard enough, but this was like facing nine at the same time. Heracles first tried to chop off the Hydra's heads, but each time he did so, two more grew to replace it. With his enemy multiplying, Heracles came up with a solution. Every time he cut through one of the Hydra's necks, his companion Iolas would hold a lighted torch to the wound to stop a new head appearing. In this way the Hydra was finally vanquished.

The poisoned arrows

As the Hydra lay dead, Heracles dipped his arrow tips in the creature's blood, which made them deadly poisonous.

Ask the storyteller

Who was Iolas?

Iolas was the son of Heracles's half-brother Iphicles, and as well as helping Heracles with his Labours, he was also said to drive Heracles's chariot for him.

The Ceryneian Deer

Seeing that Heracles had no problems killing creatures, King Eurystheus next sent the hero to capture a magical deer in the land of Ceryneia. This creature was sacred to the goddess Artemis, so it would be a great crime if Heracles were to kill it. The animal had golden antlers and hooves of bronze and people say it could run as fast as the wind. Whether this is quite true or not, Heracles chased the deer for a whole year without stopping, before finally immobilising it with an arrow in the land of Arcadia. Then, hoisting the beautiful creature on to his broad shoulders, he carried his catch back to King Eurystheus. The king demanded that Heracles dedicate it to the goddess Artemis at her temple.

A squabble with a god

When Heracles was carrying the deer back to Eurystheus, he met the god Apollo on the way. Apollo tried to take the creature from Heracles, saying that Heracles was trying to kill the sacred animal. However, Heracles managed to explain his actions and Apollo let him go on his way.

Who was the goddess Artemis?

Artemis was goddess of the Moon and hunting. She roamed the forest with a band of loyal followers – all of them female.

I hope this doesn't kill it.

The Erymanthian Boar

As his fourth labour, King Eurystheus sent Heracles to capture a ferocious boar, a kind of wild pig, which lived on Mount Erymanthus. This huge creature had long tusks coming from its mouth and a terrible temper. For years it had terrorised the local farmers, destroying their crops and goring them to death.

Heracles forced the animal into the open by shouting threats and throwing his spear, eventually chasing it to the very top of the mountain, where deep snow lay. The boar, now exhausted after the long chase, became stuck in a large snowdrift and Heracles managed to snare it in a net. He then dragged it all the way back to Mycenae. He didn't get as far as King Eurystheus's palace, however. He just dropped the trussed-up boar in the marketplace of the city and went to join another hero Jason, on his ship, the *Argo*.

A battle with the centaurs

On his way to do battle with the boar, Heracles stopped for a drink with a famous centaur called Pholus. Other centaurs were jealous and tried to kill Heracles, but he drove them off with logs from the fire.

Come on, you fat pig!

Ask the storyteller

What happened to Pholus?

While Heracles was dealing with the angry centaurs, Pholus tried to pick up the hero's bow and arrows to help. Unfortunately, one of the poisoned arrows fell on his foot and killed him.

The Stables of King Augeas

Well, Heracles had proved that he was both brave and strong, but his next task would require his wits as well. He had to clean out the stables of the King of Elis, called Augeas. This king had more cattle than anyone else in Greece, including goats, sheep, horses and cows. They were all kept together in a stable which had not been cleaned for 30 years. You can imagine the mess! And Heracles was told to complete the task in a single day!

He tackled the problem using his brain more than his brawn. He knocked two holes in opposite ends of the stables. Then, with the help of Iolas, he diverted two nearby rivers, Alpheus and Peneus, so that they flowed through the first hole and washed all the mess out through the second. So Heracles was successful without so much as dirtying his hands.

Augeas breaks the deal

King Augeas had promised that if Heracles was successful, he could keep one tenth of the cattle for himself. However, when Heracles came to claim his payment, the king refused to give him anything and said that he had never made such a bargain.

Did Heracles leave without a fight?

King Augeas should have thought twice before swindling Heracles. The hero kicked Augeas out of power and placed his son, Phyleus, on the throne instead.

The Stymphalian Birds

Heracles's sixth Labour took him to northern Greece and the land of Stymphalus. Here, above a marsh, lived a flock of birds you'd never want to come across. They were giant winged creatures, with bronze beaks and razor-sharp talons. Not surprisingly, they were sacred to the god of war and weapons, Ares, and a terror to the people who farmed in the area. When Heracles arrived he could not get close to them, because he feared treading in the marsh and drowning. Nor could he kill them straightaway with his arrows, because they cowered in the tall trees above, or the long marsh grasses below. With a little help from the gods he found the answer. Using a magical rattle, called a *krotala*, he scared the birds out of their hiding place. Then, as they flew away, he quickly shot them down one by one. The sky was full of feathers and the curse of Stymphalus was finally lifted.

Man-eaters...

...or nuisances?

Some stories say that the birds were flesh-eaters, which carried off children and animals, while others say that they were just a menace, poisoning crops with their droppings. Either way, the people who lived nearby were happy to be rid of them.

PLOP

Ask the storyteller

Where did Heracles get the rattle from?

The *krotala* were made by Hephaestus, the god of blacksmiths, who was rumoured to be very ugly. He gave them to the goddess Athena, who passed them on to Heracles.

The Cretan Bull

Heracles's seventh labour took him to the island of Crete to capture a famous bull which lived there. The animal was sacred to the god Poseidon and had an interesting history. A man called Minos had wanted to prove to the people of Crete that he was the rightful king, so he asked the gods to send him a miracle that would convince the citizens. Poseidon heard the prayer and made the bull appear out of the sea, much to the astonishment of the Cretans. However, when Minos was supposed to sacrifice the beautiful animal he refused, because he wanted to keep it for himself. His fate is another story. What we need to know is that Heracles wrestled the bull until he tired it out, then set off to show it to King Eurystheus.

The Minotaur

To punish King Minos for not sacrificing the bull, Poseidon made his wife fall in love with it. To Minos's shame, his wife Pasiphae gave birth to a child called the Minotaur, which was half-man, half-bull, and ate human flesh! Minos imprisoned this creature in a maze called the Labyrinth, where it was eventually killed by another hero, Theseus.

Ask the storyteller

What happened to the bull?

When Heracles brought the animal before Eurystheus, the king ordered that it be freed. The bull ran amok and ended up in the plain of Marathon (near Athens), where another hero, Theseus, captured it and sacrificed it to the god Apollo.

Be careful with my pet! He's used to better treatment.

The Horses of King Diomedes

By now, Eurystheus was becoming tired of Heracles's successes. He sent him on a particularly dangerous mission, hoping if he returned at least a few limbs would be missing. So Heracles travelled over the sea to Thrace, where a king named Diomedes ruled over a tribe called the Bistones. Heracles's orders were to capture the four mares which pulled Diomedes's chariot. The problem was that the horses liked the taste of human flesh and would devour anyone who came near them. People say King Diomedes kept them under control by feeding them his unsuspecting guests!

With the help of his friend Abderus, Heracles overcame the grooms who looked after the savage beasts and drove them down to the sea where his boat awaited. However, Diomedes and the Bistones gave chase and Heracles had to fight them off.

Dragged to death

While Heracles dealt with the Bistones, he put his friend Abderus in charge of the mares. Unfortunately they were too powerful for him to handle and he was pulled along the ground until he died.

Ask the storyteller

What happened to King Diomedes?

He came to a sticky end. Heracles fed the former master to his hungry horses. This magically made them tame and easy to control.

It'll be feeding time soon, Diomedes!

The Girdle of Hippolyte

Heracles's next task was of a slightly different kind. To the east of the Aegean Sea lived a band of fierce women called the Amazons. Even most men thought twice about facing them in battle. King Eurystheus ordered Heracles to fetch the girdle, a type of belt, worn by the Queen of the Amazons, Hippolyte. This was a belt used to hold her sword and spear and she would not give it up without a fight. So once again Heracles set sail with a small band of men, determined to fulfil the task.

When Heracles first met Hippolyte she fell in love with him and offered him the girdle of her own free will. However, Heracles's old enemy, the goddess Hera, stirred up hatred against him amongst the other Amazons. In the end, he and his men had to fight a bloody battle against them. Although he didn't want to, Heracles ended up killing Hippolyte with a stray arrow.

Warrior women

The Amazons hated men. They killed almost all of their male children at birth and made the rest slaves. The girls were raised to be soldiers. Amazon women were especially famous for their prowess on horseback.

Ask the storyteller

Why did Eurystheus want the girdle?

He didn't want it for himself. The king's daughter, Admete, had asked for the girdle as a gift. Eurystheus thought he may as well use Heracles to get it.

You'll wish you never messed with this woman!

The Cattle of Geryon

Heracles's next labour took him right across to the other side of the known world, to the land of Eurythia. His task was to steal the cattle of Geryon. These were strong, magical beasts, which grazed in the pastures there. Geryon was a giant with three heads, three bodies and six legs and arms, who loved his animals dearly. Some say he was the strongest person who ever lived. His herd was guarded by a shepherd called Eurytion and a snarling, two-headed dog called Orthrus. Heracles first killed these two with his club, before turning to the problem of Geryon himself. It was a very difficult fight, because the deformed giant could look in all directions at the same time. However, Heracles came up with a solution and killed him with a single arrow that pierced all three bodies through their one heart.

The Pillars of Heracles

To make his way to Eurythia, Heracles had to part the lands we now know as Africa and Europe. He built two huge pillars on either side of the strait to keep it open for his return journey.

Ask the storyteller

How did Heracles take the cattle back?

As a reward for his hard work, the Sun god, Helios, gave Heracles a great golden bowl in which to cross the sea. It was a rough ride, but he got home in the end.

The Golden Apples of the Hesperides

For Heracles's eleventh labour, he had to fetch the golden apples from a sacred garden at the ends of the Earth. The orchard was tended by the Hesperides, nymphs who were daughters of the Titan Atlas. It was also guarded by a terrible, two-headed serpent called Ladon. Heracles had no idea how he would complete the task, but on his way there he came across some unexpected help. He found a man called Prometheus, who was being punished by the Gods because he had stolen from them. Heracles freed him and in return Prometheus told the hero to seek out Atlas, who would go and get the apples for him. Heracles soon found him, but there was a problem. Atlas's job was to hold the world on his shoulders. So, while he went to fetch the apples the hero agreed to hold up the globe in the meantime.

Oh no! Not again!

Prometheus's punishment

Prometheus had stolen the gift of fire from Mount Olympus, to give to mortal men. As a punishment Zeus had chained him to a cliff, where everyday a giant eagle would come down and peck out his liver. Every night the liver grew back, so Prometheus's torture was never-ending.

Ask the storyteller

Why did Atlas have to hold up the world?

Atlas had tried to take over the world from the other gods and Zeus had punished him by making him bear the burden forever.

Keeper of the Underworld

Heracles had now been at his labours for eleven long years. His final duty was by far the most dangerous. King Eurystheus told him to descend to the Underworld, a task which few mortals had managed. And this was not all he had to do. Heracles would also have to bring back the ferocious dog, Cerberus, who guarded the dark kingdom. However, Cerberus was no ordinary dog. He had three heads, and a coat bristling with poisonous snakes.

Heracles descended into the Underworld through a cavern in a place called Taenarum. He then crossed the River Styx and visited Hades, ruler of the dead, and asked if he could take the dog away. Hades gave him permission, provided he use only his brute strength and no weapons. Heracles succeeded, but when he took the beast before Eurystheus, the king was so scared he ordered it to be returned immediately.

Rescuing an old friend

While in the Underworld, Heracles freed his friend, the hero Theseus. Theseus and his friend, Perithous, had been captured trying to free Hades's queen, Persephone, whom Hades had abducted from the land of the living.

Ask the storyteller

Is that the end?

With his 12 labours completed, Heracles had fulfilled his debt to Hera. He went on to become the most famous of all Greek heroes, celebrated in art and poetry for centuries to come.

Glossary

Abducted Taken away against one's will.

Amazons A race of warrior women.

Centaur A creature which is half-man, half-horse.

Girdle A type of belt.

Groom Someone who looks after horses.

Immobilise To make something unable to move.

Krotala A special rattle made for Heracles by the god Hephaestus.

Mortal Someone who will die one day.

Mount Olympus A place where the gods were thought to live.

Nymph A beautiful woman related to the gods.

Orchard A place where fruit trees grow.

Pelt The skin of a dead animal.

Pithos A large jar for storing food.

Prowess Skill or strength.

Quiver A container for arrows.

Ravenous Very hungry.

River Sytx A river in the Underworld.

Sacrifice To kill a creature or person as a gift to a god.

Titan One of a race of giant gods overthrown by Zeus.

Underworld The place where Ancient Greeks thought a person went after they died.

Vanquished Overcome by force.

Who's who

Abderus (ab-DE-rus) Companion of Heracles.

Admete (ad-MEET-ee) Daughter of Eurystheus.

Alcmene (alk-MEAN-uh) Mother of Heracles

Apollo (a-POLL-oh) Greek god of medicine and music.

Atlas (AT-lass) A Titan.

Ares (AIR-eez) Greek god of war.

Artemis (ARE-teem-iss) Greek goddess of hunting.

Augeas (or-JEE-ass) A king who owned thousands of cattle.

Bistones (bis-TOE-neez) The race ruled by King Diomedes.

Cerberus (KER-be-russ) The dog who guarded the Underworld.

Diomedes (die-oh-MEED-eez) A king who owned four man-eating horses.

Eurystheus (you-riss-THEY-us) The king who set Heracles's labours.

Eurytion (you-RIT-ee-on) The shepherd who guarded Geryon's cattle.

Geryon (GE-ree-on) A three headed, three-bodied giant.

Hades (HEY-deez) Greek god of the Underworld.

Helios (HEE-lee-oss) Greek sun god.

Hephaestus (heff-ICE-toss) Greek god of blacksmiths.

Hera (HEE-rah) A goddess and wife of Zeus.

Heracles (HEE-rack-leez) The most famous Greek hero.

Hesperides (hess-PE-rid-eez) Nymphs and daughters of Atlas.

Hippolyte (hip-OLL-it-ee) Queen of the Amazons.

Iphicles (IF-ick-leez) Half-brother of Heracles.

Iolas (YO-lass) Nephew of Heracles.

Jason (JAY-sun) A Greek hero who stole a famous golden fleece.

Minos (MINE-oss) King of Crete.

Minotaur (MINE-oh-tor) A creature who was half-man, half-bull.

Orthrus (OR-thruss) The two-headed dog belonging to Eurytion.

Perithous (PE-rith-oos) A Greek hero.

Persephone (per-SEF-on-ee) A goddess abducted by Hades.

Pholus (FOH-luss) A centaur.

Poseidon (poss-EYE-don) Greek god of the sea.

Prometheus (prom-EE-thee-us) A man who stole the secret of fire from the gods and gave it to mortals.

Theseus (THEE-see-us) A Greek hero.

Zeus (ZYOOS) King of the Greek gods.

Index